A Teach Me About Book

I Love Mommies and Daddies

Teach Me About I Love Mommies and Daddies

Published by Inspired Studios, Inc.
Boynton Beach, FL 33473

Published under license from Brite Star Media Group, Inc.

ISBN
Softcover 978-0-7396-0288-1

A Teach Me About Book

I Love Mommies and Daddies

Joy Berry

I love Mommy and Daddy!

In many ways, Mommy and Daddy are like me.

They have bodies that work like my body works.

Like me, Mommy and Daddy have feelings.

Sometimes they feel happy.

Sometimes they feel sad or angry.

Like me, Mommy and Daddy need to be loved.

I do things to show them that I love them.

I tell them that I love them.

In some ways my mommy and daddy are not like me.

My mommy and daddy are older than I am.

They are bigger and stronger than I am.

And they know more than I do.

My mommy and daddy
can take care of me
because they are older,
bigger, stronger, and
know more than I do.

My mommy and daddy take care of me by making sure that I get all the things I need.

My mommy and daddy
take care of me by
helping me stay safe
and well.

My mommy and daddy take care of me by telling me what to do so I will not hurt myself or others.

My mommy and daddy tell me “no” so I will not damage or destroy things.

Mommy and Daddy love me and take care of me.

I love Mommy and Daddy!